oa

Mary Elizabeth Salzmann

Published by SandCastle™, an imprint of ABDO Publishing Company, 4940 Viking Drive, Edina, Minnesota 55435.

Printed in the United States.

Cover and interior photo credits: Comstock, Corbis Images, Eyewire Images, PhotoDisc, Stockbyte

Library of Congress Cataloging-in-Publication Data

Salzmann, Mary Elizabeth, 1968-
    Oa / Mary Elizabeth Salzmann.
      p. cm. -- (Vowel blends)
    ISBN 1-57765-456-0
    1. Readers (Primary) [1. English language--Phonetics.] I. Title.

PE1119 .S234237 2001
428.1--dc21
                                                                        00-056567

The SandCastle concept, content, and reading method have been reviewed and approved by a national advisory board including literacy specialists, librarians, elementary school teachers, early childhood education professionals, and parents.

Let Us Know

After reading the book, SandCastle would like you to tell us your stories about reading. What is your favorite page? Was there something hard that you needed help with? Share the ups and downs of learning to read. We want to hear from you! To get posted on the ABDO Publishing Company Web site, send us email at:

sandcastle@abdopub.com

About SandCastle™

Nonfiction books for the beginning reader

- Basic concepts of phonics are incorporated with integrated language methods of reading instruction. Most words are short, and phrases, letter sounds, and word sounds are repeated.

- Readability is determined by the number of words in each sentence, the number of characters in each word, and word lists based on curriculum frameworks.

- Full-color photography reinforces word meanings and concepts.

- "Words I Can Read" list at the end of each book teaches basic elements of grammar, helps the reader recognize the words in the text, and builds vocabulary.

- Reading levels are indicated by the number of flags on the castle.

Look for more SandCastle books in these three reading levels:

Level 1 (one flag)	**Level 2** (two flags)	**Level 3** (three flags)

Grades Pre-K to K 5 or fewer words per page	**Grades K to 1** 5 to 10 words per page	**Grades 1 to 2** 10 to 15 words per page

Roarke and Noam have fun sailing their boat.

They hope it will stay afloat.

Sloan likes to play soccer.

He is about to score a goal.

Sloane wears her coat and drinks hot cocoa to stay warm.

Joan and her mom roast marshmallows over a roaring campfire.

Joanie likes to eat toast with butter and jam for breakfast.

Joaquin is good at math.
He does a problem on the
chalkboard.

oa

Moana and Noami take a walk along the coast with their parents.

17

Oakes has a frog on
his hat.

It makes a loud croak.

Oakley feeds his pets hay and oats.

What kind of animals are they?

(goats)

Words I Can Read

Nouns

A noun is a person, place, or thing

animals (AN-uh-muhlz)
p. 21

boat (BOTE) p. 5

breakfast (BREK-fuhst)
p. 13

butter (BUHT-ur) p. 13

campfire (KAMP-fire)
p. 11

chalkboard
(CHAWK-bord) p. 15

coast (KOHST) p. 17

coat (KOHT) p. 9

cocoa (KOH-koh) p. 9

croak (KROHK) p. 19

frog (FROG) p. 19

fun (FUHN) p. 5

goal (GOHL) p. 7

goats (GOHTSS) p. 21

hat (HAT) p. 19

hay (HAY) p. 21

jam (JAM) p. 13

kind (KINDE) p. 21

marshmallows
(MARSH-mal-lohz)
p. 11

math (MATH) p. 15

mom (MOM) p. 11

oats (OHTSS) p. 21

parents (PAIR-uhntss)
p. 17

pets (PETSS) p. 21

problem (PROB-luhm)
p. 15

soccer (SOK-ur) p. 7

toast (TOHST) p. 13

walk (WAWK) p. 17

Proper Nouns

A proper noun is the name
of a person, place, or thing

Joan (JOHN) p. 11

Joanie (JOH-nee) p. 13

Joaquin (YOH-kwin)
p. 15

Moana (MOH-nuh)
p. 17

Noam (NOHM) p. 5

Noami (NOH-mee)
p. 17

Oakes (OHKSS) p. 19

Oakley (OHK-lee) p. 21

Roarke (ROHRK) p. 5

Sloan (SLOHN) p. 7

Sloane (SLOHN) p. 9

Pronouns

A pronoun is a word that replaces a noun

he (HEE) pp. 7, 15   **they** (THAY) pp. 5, 21   **what** (WUHT) p. 21
it (IT) pp. 5, 19

Verbs

A verb is an action or being word

are (AR) p. 21   **hope** (HOPE) p. 5   **score** (SKOR) p. 7
does (DUHZ) p. 15   **is** (IZ) pp. 7, 15   **stay** (STAY) pp. 5, 9
drinks (DRINGKSS) p. 9 **likes** (LIKESS) pp. 7, 13 **take** (TAYK) p. 17
eat (EET) p. 13   **makes** (MAKESS) p. 19   **wears** (WAIRZ) p. 9
feeds (FEEDZ) p. 21   **play** (PLAY) p. 7   **will** (WIL) p. 5
has (HAZ) p. 19   **roast** (ROHST) p. 11
have (HAV) p. 5   **sailing** (SAYL-ing) p. 5

Adjectives

An adjective describes something

afloat (uh-FLOTE) p. 5 **his** (HIZ) pp. 19, 21   **roaring** (ROR-ing) p. 11
good (GUD) p. 15   **hot** (HOT) p. 9   **their** (THAIR) pp. 5, 17
her (HUR) pp. 9, 11   **loud** (LOUD) p. 19   **warm** (WORM) p. 9

Adverbs

An adverb tells how, when, or where something happens

about (uh-BOUT) p. 7

23

Glossary

campfire – A fire lit at the site of a camp for warmth and cooking.

chalkboard – A hard, smooth, slate surface you write on with chalk.

coast – The land that is next to a sea or ocean

marshmallows – A soft, spongy kind of white candy.

More oa Words

approach	groan	oar
boar	hoarse	road
coal	loaf	roar
foal	loan	soap
foam	moat	throat